Contents

Acknowledgements

AUTHOR

Stuart Rance, HP

KEY ELEMENT GUIDE AUTHORING TEAM

David Cannon, BMC Software

Ashley Hanna, HP

Lou Hunnebeck, Third Sky Inc.

Vernon Lloyd, Fox IT

Randy Steinberg, Migration Technologies Inc.

REVIEWERS

Best Management Practice and The Stationery Office would like to thank itSMF International for managing the quality assurance of this publication, and the following reviewers for their contributions:

Duncan Anderson, Global Knowledge; John Donoghue, Allied Irish Bank plc; John Earle, itSMF Ireland Ltd; Robert Falkowitz, Concentric Circle Consulting; Padraig Farrell, SureSkills; Siobhan Flaherty, Generali PanEurope; Signe Marie Hernes Bjerke, Det Norske Veritas; Michael Imhoff Nielsen, IBM; Jackie Manning, Bord Gáis Networks; Krikor Maroukian, King's College London; Reiko Morita, Ability InterBusiness Solutions Inc.; Trevor Murray, The Grey Matters; Gary O'Dwyer, Allied Irish Banks plc; Benjamin Orazem, SRC d.o.o.; Sue Shaw, TriCentrica; Marco Smith, iCore Ltd; Hon P Suen, ECT Service Ltd; and Paul Wigzel, Paul Wigzel Training and Consultancy.

1   Introduction

This key element guide is intended to provide a summary of the basic concepts and practice elements of *ITIL Service Transition*, which forms part of the core ITIL publication suite.

ITIL is a set of best-practice publications for IT service management (ITSM).[1] ITIL provides guidance on the provision of quality IT services, and on the capabilities needed to support them. ITIL is not a standard that has to be followed; it is guidance that should be read and understood, and used to create value for the service provider and its customers. Organizations are encouraged to adopt ITIL best practices and to adapt them to work in their specific environments in ways that meet their needs.

ITIL is the most widely recognized framework for ITSM in the world. In the 20 years since it was created, ITIL has evolved and changed its breadth and depth as technologies and business practices have developed.

The section numbering in this key element guide is not the same as the section numbers in the core publication, *ITIL Service Transition*. Therefore, do not try to use references to section numbers in the core publication when referencing material in this key element guide.

1.1   THE ITIL SERVICE LIFECYCLE

The ITIL framework is based on five stages of the service lifecycle as shown in Figure 1.1, with a core publication providing best-practice guidance for each stage. This guidance includes principles, processes and activities, organization and roles, technology, challenges, critical success factors, and risks. The service lifecycle uses a hub-and-spoke

---

[1] ITSM and other concepts from this chapter are described in more detail in Chapter 2.

Figure 1.1 The ITIL service lifecycle

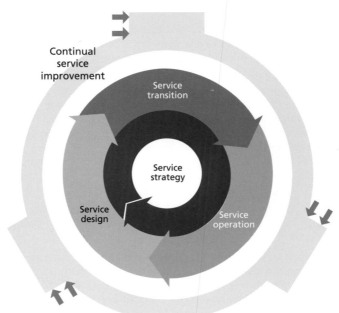

design, with service strategy at the hub, and service design, service transition and service operation as the revolving lifecycle stages or 'spokes'. Continual service improvement surrounds and supports all stages of the service lifecycle. Each stage of the lifecycle exerts influence on the others and relies on them for inputs and feedback. In this way, a constant set of checks and balances ensures that as business demand changes, the services can adapt and respond effectively.

In addition to the core publications, there is also a complementary set of ITIL publications providing guidance specific to industry sectors, organization types, operating models and technology architectures.

The following key characteristics of ITIL contribute to its global success:

- **Vendor-neutral** ITIL service management practices are not based on any particular technology platform or industry type. ITIL is owned by the UK government and is not tied to any commercial proprietary practice or solution.
- **Non-prescriptive** ITIL offers robust, mature and time-tested practices that have applicability to all types of service organization. It continues to be useful and relevant in public and private sectors, internal and external service providers, small, medium and large enterprises, and within any technical environment.
- **Best practice** ITIL represents the learning experiences and thought leadership of the world's best-in-class service providers.

1.2   SERVICE TRANSITION – KEY ELEMENT GUIDE

ITIL Service Transition provides best-practice guidance for the service transition stage of the service lifecycle.

1.2.1   Purpose and objectives of service transition

The purpose of the service transition stage of the service lifecycle is to ensure that new, modified or retired services meet the expectations of the business as documented in the service strategy and service design stages of the lifecycle.

The objectives of service transition are to:

- Plan and manage service changes efficiently and effectively
- Manage risks relating to new, changed or retired services
- Successfully deploy service releases into supported environments
- Set correct expectations on the performance and use of new or changed services
- Ensure that service changes create the expected business value
- Provide good-quality knowledge and information about services and service assets.

1.2.2 Scope

ITIL Service Transition provides guidance for the development and improvement of capabilities for transitioning new and changed services into supported environments. The publication also considers service retirement, transfer of services between service providers, and the transition of changes in the service provider's service management capabilities.

The processes described in *ITIL Service Transition* can be categorized into two groups, based on the extent to which process activities take place within the service transition stage of the service lifecycle.

Some processes influence and support all stages of the service lifecycle:

- Change management
- Service asset and configuration management (SACM)
- Knowledge management.

Other processes are strongly focused within the service transition stage:

- Transition planning and support
- Release and deployment management
- Service testing and validation
- Change evaluation.

Some activities of all service transition processes may be carried out during the service design stage of the service lifecycle – for example, design of a release package or planning of a service transition.

1.2.3 Value to business

Adopting and implementing standard and consistent approaches for service transition will:

- Enable projects to estimate the cost, timing, resource requirement and risks associated with the service transition stage more accurately
- Result in higher volumes of successful change
- Improve expectation-setting for all stakeholders involved in service transition
- Ensure that new or changed services will be maintainable and cost-effective.

1.3 CONTEXT

Each core ITIL publication addresses those capabilities that have a direct impact on a service provider's performance. The core is expected to provide structure, stability and strength to service management capabilities, with durable principles, methods and tools. This serves to protect investments and provide the necessary basis for measurement, learning and improvement.

1.3.1 Service strategy

At the centre of the service lifecycle is service strategy. Value creation begins here with understanding organizational objectives and customer needs. Every organizational asset, including people, processes and products, should support the strategy.

ITIL Service Strategy provides guidance on how to view service management not only as an organizational capability but as a strategic asset. It describes the principles underpinning the practice of service management which are useful for developing service management policies, guidelines and processes across the service lifecycle.

Organizations already practising ITIL can use *ITIL Service Strategy* to guide a strategic review of their service management capabilities and to improve the alignment between those capabilities and their business strategies. *ITIL Service Strategy* will encourage readers to stop and think about *why* something is to be done before thinking of *how*.

1.3.2 Service design
Service design is the stage in the lifecycle that turns a service strategy into a plan for delivering business objectives. *ITIL Service Design* provides guidance for the design and development of services and service management practices. It covers design principles and methods for converting strategic objectives into portfolios of services and service assets. The scope of *ITIL Service Design* includes the changes and improvements necessary to increase or maintain value to customers over the lifecycle of services, the continuity of services, the achievement of service levels, and conformance to standards and regulations.

1.3.3 Service transition
ITIL Service Transition provides guidance for the development and improvement of capabilities for introducing new and changed services into supported environments. It describes how to transition an organization from one state to another while controlling risk and supporting organizational knowledge for decision support. It ensures

that the value(s) identified in the service strategy, and encoded in the service design, are effectively transitioned so that they can be realized in service operation.

1.3.4 Service operation

ITIL Service Operation describes best practice for managing services in supported environments. It includes guidance on achieving effectiveness and efficiency in the delivery and support of services to ensure value for the customer, the users and the service provider. *ITIL Service Operation* provides guidance on how to maintain stability in service operation, even while allowing for changes in design, scale, scope and service levels.

1.3.5 Continual service improvement

ITIL Continual Service Improvement provides guidance on creating and maintaining value for customers through better strategy, design, transition and operation of services. It combines principles, practices and methods from quality management, change management and capability improvement.

ITIL Continual Service Improvement describes best practice for achieving incremental and large-scale improvements in service quality, operational efficiency and business continuity, and for ensuring that the service portfolio continues to be aligned to business needs.

2   Service management as a practice

2.1   SERVICES AND SERVICE MANAGEMENT

2.1.1   Services

Definitions

Service: A means of delivering value to customers by facilitating outcomes customers want to achieve without the ownership of specific costs and risks.

IT service: A service provided by an IT service provider. An IT service is made up of a combination of information technology, people and processes. A customer-facing IT service directly supports the business processes of one or more customers and its service level targets should be defined in a service level agreement. Other IT services, called supporting services, are not directly used by the business but are required by the service provider to deliver customer-facing services.

Outcome: The result of carrying out an activity, following a process, or delivering an IT service etc. The term is used to refer to intended results, as well as to actual results.

An outcome-based definition of service moves IT organizations beyond business–IT alignment towards business–IT integration. Customers seek outcomes but do not wish to have accountability or ownership of all the associated costs and risks. The customer can judge the value of a service based on a comparison of cost or price and reliability with the desired outcome. Customer satisfaction is also important. Customer expectations keep shifting, and a service provider that does not track this will soon lose business.

2.1.2 Service management

Business would like IT services to behave like other utilities such as water, electricity or the telephone. Simply having the best technology does not ensure that the IT service will provide utility-like reliability. Service management can bring this utility quality of service to the business.

> **Definitions**
>
> *Service management:* A set of specialized organizational capabilities for providing value to customers in the form of services.
>
> *Service provider:* An organization supplying services to one or more internal or external customers.

The more mature a service provider's capabilities are, the greater is their ability to meet the needs of the customer. The act of transforming capabilities and resources into valuable services is at the core of service management. The origins of service management are in traditional service businesses such as airlines, banks and hotels.

2.1.3 IT service management

Every IT organization should act as a service provider, using service management to ensure that they deliver outcomes required by their customers. A service level agreement (SLA) is used to document agreements between an IT service provider and a customer. An SLA describes the service, documents targets, and specifies the responsibilities of the service provider and the customer.

2.1.4 Service providers

There are three main types of service provider:

- **Type I – internal service provider** This type is embedded within a business unit. There may be several Type I service providers within an organization.
- **Type II – shared services unit** An internal service provider that provides shared IT services to more than one business unit.
- **Type III – external service provider** A service provider that provides IT services to external customers.

IT service management (ITSM) concepts are often described in the context of only one of these types. In reality most organizations have a combination of IT service provider types.

2.1.5 Stakeholders in service management

Stakeholders have an interest in an organization, project or service etc. and may also be interested in the activities, targets, resources or deliverables. There are many stakeholders inside the service provider. There are also many external stakeholders, for example:

- **Customers** Those who buy goods or services. Customers define and agree the service level targets.
- **Users** Those who use the service on a day-to-day basis.
- **Suppliers** Third parties responsible for supplying goods or services that are required to deliver IT services.

There is a difference between internal customers and external customers:

- **Internal customers** These work for the same business as the service provider – for example, the marketing department uses IT services.
- **External customers** These work for a different business from the service provider. External customers typically purchase services by means of a legally binding contract or agreement.

2.1.6 Utility and warranty

From the customer's perspective, value consists of achieving business objectives. The value of a service is created by combining utility (fitness for purpose) and warranty (fitness for use).

- **Utility** is the ability to meet a particular need. It is often described as 'what the service does' – for example, a service that enables a business unit to process orders.
- **Warranty** is an assurance that the service will meet its agreed requirements. Warranty includes the ability of a service to be available when needed, to provide the required capacity, and to provide the required reliability in terms of continuity and security.

The value of a service is only created when both utility and warranty are designed and delivered.

Information about the desired business outcomes, opportunities, customers, utility and warranty of the service is used to develop the definition of a service. Using an outcome-based definition helps to ensure that managers plan and execute all aspects of service management from the customer's perspective.

2.1.7 Best practices in the public domain

Organizations benchmark themselves against peers and seek to close gaps in capabilities. This enables them to become more competitive. One way to close gaps is the adoption of best practices. There are several sources for best practice including public frameworks, standards and the proprietary knowledge of organizations and individuals. ITIL is the most widely recognized and trusted source of best-practice guidance for ITSM.

2.2 BASIC CONCEPTS

2.2.1 Assets, resources and capabilities

The relationship between service providers and customers revolves around the use of assets – both those of the service provider and those of the customer. The performance of customer assets is a primary concern for service management.

> **Definitions**
>
> *Asset:* Any resource or capability.
>
> *Customer asset:* Any resource or capability used by a customer to achieve a business outcome.
>
> *Service asset:* Any resource or capability used by a service provider to deliver services to a customer.

There are two types of asset – resources and capabilities. Resources are direct inputs for production. Capabilities represent an organization's ability to coordinate, control and deploy resources to produce value. It is relatively easy to acquire resources compared to capabilities. Figure 2.1 shows examples of capabilities and resources.

2.2.2 Processes

> **Definition: process**
>
> A process is a structured set of activities designed to accomplish a specific objective. A process takes one or more defined inputs and turns them into defined outputs.

Figure 2.1 Examples of capabilities and resources

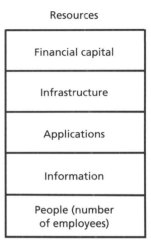

Capabilities	Resources
Management	Financial capital
Organization	Infrastructure
Processes	Applications
Knowledge	Information
People (experience, skills and relationships)	People (number of employees)

Process characteristics include:

- **Measurability** We can measure the process in a relevant manner.
- **Specific results** The process delivers specific results, which must be individually identifiable and countable.
- **Customers** The process delivers its primary results to a customer or stakeholder. Customers may be internal or external to the organization.
- **Responsiveness to specific triggers** The process should be traceable to a specific trigger.

The outputs from the process should be driven by the process objectives. Process measurement and metrics can be built into the process to control and improve the process as illustrated in Figure 2.2.

Figure 2.2 Process model

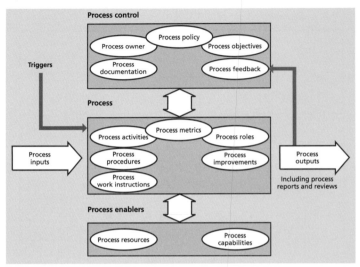

2.2.3 Organizing for service management

Best practices described in ITIL need to be tailored to suit organizations and situations. The starting point for organizational design is service strategy.

2.2.3.1 Functions

A function is a team or group of people and the tools or other resources they use to carry out one or more processes or activities. In larger organizations, a function may be performed by several departments, teams and groups. In smaller organizations, one person or group can perform multiple functions – for example, a technical management department could also incorporate the service desk function.

ITIL Service Operation describes the following functions:

- **Service desk** The single point of contact for users. A typical service desk manages incidents and service requests, and also handles communication with the users.
- **Technical management** Provides technical skills and resources needed to manage the IT infrastructure throughout the service lifecycle.
- **IT operations management** Executes the daily operational activities needed to manage IT services and the supporting IT infrastructure.
- **Application management** Is responsible for managing applications throughout their lifecycle. This differs from application development which is mainly concerned with one-time activities for requirements, design and build of applications.

The other core ITIL publications rely on the technical and application management functions described in *ITIL Service Operation*, but they do not define any additional functions in detail.

2.2.3.2 Roles

The core ITIL publications provide guidelines and examples of role descriptions. In many cases roles will need to be combined or separated.

Definition: role

A role is a set of responsibilities, activities and authorities granted to a person or team. A role is defined in a process or function. One person or team may have multiple roles – for example, the roles of configuration manager and change manager may be carried out by a single person.

Roles are often confused with job titles but they are not the same. Each organization defines job titles and job descriptions, and individuals holding these job titles can perform one or more roles. See Chapter 5 for more details about roles and responsibilities.

2.2.4 The service portfolio

The service portfolio is the complete set of services managed by a service provider, and it represents the service provider's commitments and investments across all customers and market spaces. It consists of three parts:

■ **Service pipeline** Services that are under consideration or development, but are not yet available to customers. The service pipeline is a service provider's business view of possible future services.
■ **Service catalogue** Live IT services, including those available for deployment. It is the only part of the service portfolio that is published to customers. It includes a customer-facing view (or views) of the IT services. It also includes information about supporting services required by the service provider.
■ **Retired services** Services that have retired.

Service providers often find it useful to distinguish customer-facing services from supporting services:

■ **Customer-facing services** are visible to the customer. These normally support the customer's business processes and facilitate outcomes desired by the customer.
■ **Supporting services** support or 'underpin' the customer-facing services. These are typically invisible to the customer, but are essential to the delivery of customer-facing services.

Figure 2.3 illustrates the components of the service portfolio. These are important components of the service knowledge management system (SKMS) described in section 2.2.5.

Figure 2.3 The service portfolio and its contents

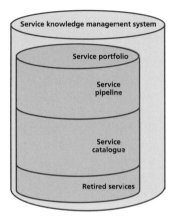

2.2.5 Knowledge management and the SKMS

Knowledge and information enable people to perform activities and support information flow between lifecycle stages and processes. Implementing knowledge management enables effective decision support and reduces risks.

ITIL Service Transition describes an architecture for a service knowledge management system (SKMS) with four layers:

- **Presentation layer** Enables searching, browsing, retrieving, updating, subscribing and collaboration. Different views are provided for different audiences.
- **Knowledge-processing layer** Where information is converted into knowledge which enables decision-making.
- **Information integration layer** Provides integrated information from data in multiple sources in the data layer.

■ **Data layer** Includes tools for data discovery and collection, and data items in unstructured and structured forms.

2.3 GOVERNANCE AND MANAGEMENT SYSTEMS

2.3.1 Governance

Governance defines the common directions, policies and rules that both the business and IT use to conduct business.

> **Definition: governance**
>
> Ensures that policies and strategy are actually implemented, and that required processes are correctly followed. Governance includes defining roles and responsibilities, measuring and reporting, and taking actions to resolve any issues identified.

Governance applies a consistently managed approach at all levels of the organization by ensuring a clear strategy is set, and by defining the policies needed to achieve the strategy.

2.3.2 Management systems

Many businesses have adopted management system standards for competitive advantage, to ensure a consistent approach in implementing service management, and to support governance.

An organization can adopt multiple management system standards, such as:

■ A quality management system (ISO 9001)
■ An environmental management system (ISO 14000)
■ A service management system (ISO/IEC 20000)
■ An information security management system (ISO/IEC 27001)
■ A management system for software asset management (ISO/IEC 19770).

Figure 2.4 Plan-Do-Check-Act cycle

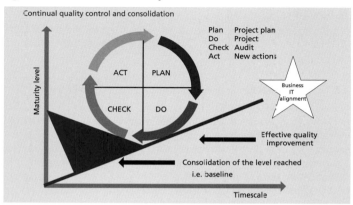

As there are common elements between such management systems, they should be managed in an integrated way rather than having separate management systems.

ISO management system standards use the Plan-Do-Check-Act (PDCA) cycle shown in Figure 2.4. This PDCA cycle is used in each of the core ITIL publications.

> **Definition: ISO/IEC 20000**
>
> An international standard for IT service management.

ISO/IEC 20000 is an international standard that allows organizations to prove best practice in ITSM. Part 1 specifies requirements for the service provider to plan, establish, implement, operate, monitor, review, maintain and improve a service management system (SMS). One of the most common routes for an organization to achieve the requirements of ISO/IEC 20000 is by adopting ITIL.

2.4 THE SERVICE LIFECYCLE

The service lifecycle is an organizing framework, supported by the organizational structure, service portfolio and service models within an organization. See Chapter 1 for an introduction to each ITIL service lifecycle stage.

2.4.1 Specialization and coordination across the lifecycle

Organizations should function in the same manner as a high-performing sports team. Each player in a team and each member of the team's organization who are not players position themselves to support the goal of the team. Each player and team member has a different specialization that contributes to the whole. The team matures over time taking into account feedback from experience, best practice and current processes and procedures to become an agile high-performing team.

Specialization allows for expert focus on components of the service but components of the service also need to work together for value. Coordination across the lifecycle creates an environment focused on business and customer outcomes instead of just IT objectives and projects. Specialization combined with coordination helps to manage expertise, improve focus and reduce overlaps and gaps in processes.

Adopting technology to automate the processes and provide management information that supports the processes is also important for effective and efficient service management.

2.4.2 Processes through the service lifecycle

Each core ITIL publication includes guidance on service management processes as shown in Table 2.1.

Table 2.1 The processes described in each core ITIL publication

Core ITIL lifecycle publication	Processes described in the publication
ITIL Service Strategy	Strategy management for IT services
	Service portfolio management
	Financial management for IT services
	Demand management
	Business relationship management
ITIL Service Design	Design coordination
	Service catalogue management
	Service level management
	Availability management
	Capacity management
	IT service continuity management
	Information security management
	Supplier management
ITIL Service Transition	Transition planning and support
	Change management
	Service asset and configuration management
	Release and deployment management
	Service validation and testing
	Change evaluation
	Knowledge management

Table continues

Table 2.1 *continued*

Core ITIL lifecycle publication	Processes described in the publication
ITIL Service Operation	Event management
	Incident management
	Request fulfilment
	Problem management
	Access management
ITIL Continual Service improvement	Seven-step improvement process

Most ITIL roles, processes and functions have activities that take place across multiple stages of the service lifecycle. For example:

■ Service validation and testing may design tests during the service design stage and perform these tests during service transition
■ Technical management provides input to strategic decisions about technology, and assists in the design and transition of infrastructure
■ Business relationship managers assist in gathering requirements during the service design stage of the lifecycle, and take part in the management of major incidents during the service operation stage.

The strength of the service lifecycle relies on continual feedback throughout each stage of the lifecycle. At every point in the service lifecycle, monitoring, assessment and feedback drives decisions about the need for minor course corrections or major service improvement initiatives.

3 Service transition principles

3.1 POLICIES FOR SERVICE TRANSITION

Every service provider should agree and document policies such as:

- Define and implement a formal policy for service transition
- Implement all changes through service transition
- Adopt a common framework and standards
- Maximize re-use of processes and systems
- Align service transition plans with business needs
- Establish and maintain relationships with stakeholders
- Establish effective controls and disciplines
- Provide systems for knowledge transfer and decision support
- Plan release packages
- Anticipate and manage course corrections
- Proactively manage resources across service transitions
- Ensure early involvement in the service lifecycle
- Provide assurance of the quality of new or changed services
- Proactively improve quality during service transition.

3.2 OPTIMIZING SERVICE TRANSITION PERFORMANCE

Service transition must focus on delivering what the business needs within financial and other constraints. Typical metrics for measuring this are:

- Increased percentage of service plans aligned with business strategies and plans
- Percentage of customers and stakeholders that understand service transition
- Quality rating of service transition plans
- Percentage of planning meetings where stakeholders have participated

- Percentage of transition plans that are aligned with policies
- Percentage of projects that adopt service transition practices
- Percentage of release-planning documents quality assured by service transition staff.

Metrics for measuring the service transition lifecycle stage should be aligned with metrics for service design, and should consider:

- Resource utilization against capacity
- Capabilities, warranties and service levels
- Cost against budget
- Time, quality and value
- Errors and incidents
- Risks.

Examples of other metrics for optimizing service transition performance are:

- Cost of testing versus cost of incidents
- Delays caused by service transition
- Operational problems that could have been identified by service transition
- Stakeholder satisfaction
- Reduction in emergency, urgent or late changes and releases
- Reduced cost of transitioning services and releases
- Increased re-use and sharing of service assets
- More motivated staff and improved job satisfaction
- Improved communications and inter-team working
- Enhanced performance of service transition processes.

3.3   MANAGING PEOPLE THROUGH SERVICE TRANSITIONS

Service transition is not just about technology and processes. Effective service transition enables the service provider, and its customer, to use and operate new and changed services to create value. This requires the service provider to develop capabilities in communications and in managing organizational and stakeholder change.

3.3.1   Communications

Communication is central to any service transition change process. The greater the change, the greater the need for clear communication about the reasons and rationale behind it, the benefits expected, the plans for its implementation and its proposed effects. Communications need to be timely, targeted at the right audience and clearly communicate the messages and benefits consistently.

3.3.2   Managing organizational and stakeholder change

Organizational change efforts fail or fall short of their goals because changes and transitions are not led, managed and monitored efficiently across the organization and throughout the change process. These gaps in key organizational activities often result in resistance, dissatisfaction and increased costs. Change is never easy; it usually takes longer than planned and creates barriers and resistance along the way. Effective leaders and managers understand the change process and plan and lead accordingly.

There are five important ingredients of change: necessity, vision, plan, resources and competence. If there is no necessity established, there is a lot of resistance from people; if there is no vision, there is confusion among the employees; if there is no plan, there is chaos in the activities and transition; if there are no/few resources, there is a frustration among the employees; and if there is no competence, there is a fear of failure among employees. Therefore, it is extremely important to pay adequate attention and establish management commitment to take adequate care of these requirements of the change.

3.4 SERVICE TRANSITION INPUTS AND OUTPUTS

The main input to service transition is a service design package (SDP), which includes all of the information needed to manage the entire lifecycle of a new or changed service. The main output is the deployment into live use of a new or changed service, with all the supporting knowledge and information, tools and processes required to support the service.

4 Service transition processes

4.1 TRANSITION PLANNING AND SUPPORT

4.1.1 Purpose and objectives

The purpose of the transition planning and support process is to provide overall planning for service transitions, and to coordinate the resources that they require.

The objectives of transition planning and support are to:

- Plan and coordinate resources to ensure that requirements of service strategy encoded in service design are realized in service operation
- Coordinate activities across projects, suppliers and service teams
- Establish new or changed services within predicted cost, quality and time
- Establish new or modified management information systems and tools, technology and management architectures, service management processes, and measurement methods and metrics to meet agreed requirements
- Enable projects to align with service transition plans
- Identify, manage and control risks
- Monitor and improve the performance of the service transition lifecycle stage.

4.1.2 Scope

The scope of transition planning and support includes:

- Maintaining policies, standards and models for service transition
- Guiding each major change through service transition
- Coordinating efforts needed to manage multiple transitions at the same time

- Prioritizing conflicting requirements for service transition resources
- Planning service transition budget and resources
- Coordinating with programme and project management, service design and service development.

4.1.3 Value to business

Transition planning and support can improve the ability to handle high volumes of change and releases, and improve alignment with customers, suppliers and business plans.

4.1.4 Policies, principles and basic concepts

Design coordination will develop an SDP for each new or changed service. This will include:

- The service charter, describing utility, warranty, outline budgets and timescales
- Service specifications and service models
- The architectural design, including constraints
- Definition and design of each release
- Release and deployment management plans
- Service acceptance criteria (SAC).

A release policy should be defined for one or more services, including:

- Unique identification, numbering and naming conventions
- Roles and responsibilities
- Expected frequency for each release type
- Approach for grouping changes into releases
- Mechanism to automate build, installation and deployment
- How the configuration baseline is captured and verified
- Exit and entry criteria and authority for acceptance into each stage.

Types of release should be defined. A typical example is:

- **Major release** Normally contains large areas of new functionality
- **Minor release** Normally contains small enhancements and fixes
- **Emergency release** Normally contains corrections to known errors.

4.1.5 Process activities, methods and techniques

4.1.5.1 Transition strategy

The service transition strategy defines the overall approach to organizing service transition and allocating resources.

4.1.5.2 Service transition lifecycle stages

The SDP should define the stages for the transition. For each stage there will be exit and entry criteria and mandatory deliverables. Typical stages include:

- Acquire and test new configuration items (CIs) and components
- Build and test
- Service release test
- Service operational readiness test
- Deployment
- Early life support
- Review and close service transition.

4.1.5.3 Prepare for service transition

Service transition preparation activities include:

- Acceptance of inputs from other service lifecycle stages
- Reviewing and checking the input deliverables, including the SDP
- Raising requests for change (RFCs)
- Checking that baselines are recorded in the configuration management system (CMS).

4.1.5.4 Plan and coordinate service transition

Release and deployment management should be planned in stages, as details might not be known initially. The plan should be developed from a model and include:

- Work environment and infrastructure for the service transition
- Schedule of milestones, handover and delivery dates
- Activities and tasks
- Staffing, resource requirements, budgets and timescales
- Issues and risks
- Lead times and contingency.

4.1.5.5 Provide transition process support

Transition planning and support also provides support for all of the service transition processes. This includes advice, communication, and progress monitoring and reporting.

4.1.6 Triggers, inputs, outputs and interfaces

The trigger for a transition is an authorized change. Longer-term planning may be triggered by a change proposal.

Inputs to transition planning and support include:

- Change proposal
- Authorized change
- SDP.

Outputs from transition planning and support include:

- Transition strategy and budget
- Integrated set of service transition plans.

Transition planning and support has interfaces to almost every other area of service management:

- **Demand management** Provides information for longer-term planning

- **Service portfolio management (SPM)** Submits change proposals to trigger planning
- **Business relationship management** Helps to manage communication with customers
- **All service design processes** Contribute to the contents of SDPs
- **All service transition processes** Coordinated by transition planning and support. Pilots, handover and early life support must be coordinated with service operation functions
- **Technical management and application management** Provide personnel, for example to review changes or plan deployments
- **Project and programme management** Work closely with transition planning and support
- **Customers** Involved in many aspects of service transition.

4.1.7 Critical success factors and key performance indicators

Examples of critical success factors (CSFs) and key performance indicators (KPIs) for transition planning and support include:

- **CSF** Understanding and managing trade-offs between cost, quality and time
  - **KPI** Increase in number of releases that meet customer's requirements
  - **KPI** Reduced variation of actual versus predicted scope, quality, cost and time
- **CSF** Effective communication with stakeholders
  - **KPI** Increased customer and user satisfaction
- **CSF** Identifying and managing risks of failure and disruption
  - **KPI** Improved service transition success rates.

4.1.8 Challenges and risks

The biggest challenge is building up the relationships needed to manage and coordinate stakeholders. Coordinating and prioritizing many new or changed services can also be a big challenge, especially if there are delays or test failures.

Risks to transition planning and support include:

- Lack of information from demand management and SPM, resulting in insufficient planning
- Poor relationships with project and programme teams resulting in unexpected requirements
- Delays to one transition having an effect on future transitions
- Insufficient information to prioritize conflicting requirements.

4.2 CHANGE MANAGEMENT

4.2.1 Purpose and objectives

The purpose of the change management process is to control the lifecycle of all changes, enabling beneficial changes to be made with minimum disruption to IT services.

The objectives of change management are to:

- Respond to changing business requirements while maximizing value and reducing incidents and re-work
- Respond to RFCs that will align services with business needs
- Ensure that changes are recorded and evaluated, and that authorized changes are managed in a controlled manner
- Optimize overall business risk.

4.2.2 Scope

The scope of change management should include changes to all architectures, processes, tools, metrics and documentation, as well as changes to all CIs across the whole service lifecycle. It also covers all changes to any of the five aspects of service design:

- Service solutions for new or changed services
- Management information systems and tools
- Technology architectures and management architectures
- Processes
- Measurement systems, methods and metrics.

Each organization should define its own scope, typically excluding business changes such as department reorganizations and operational changes such as printer repairs.

4.2.3 Value to business

Change management enables the service provider to add value to the business by:

- Protecting the business, and other services, while making required changes
- Implementing changes that meet customers' service requirements while optimizing costs
- Contributing to governance, legal, contractual and regulatory requirements
- Reducing the number of failed and unauthorized changes
- Liaising with the business to identify opportunities for business improvement.

4.2.4 Policies, principles and basic concepts

4.2.4.1 Policies

Policies that support change management include:

- Creating a culture of change management
- Aligning with business, project and stakeholder change management
- Ensuring that changes create business value
- Establishing a single focal point for changes

■ Performance and risk evaluation of all changes that impact service capability.

4.2.4.2 Types of change request

There are three different types of service change:

■ **Standard change** A pre-authorized change that is low risk, relatively common and follows a procedure or work instruction
■ **Emergency change** A change that must be implemented as soon as possible, for example to resolve a major incident or implement a security patch
■ **Normal change** Any service change that is not a standard change or an emergency change.

Changes are often categorized as major, significant and minor, depending on the cost, risk and scope. This categorization may be used to identify an appropriate change authority.

4.2.4.3 Changes, RFCs and change records

ITIL Service Transition uses these terms as follows:

■ **Change** The addition, modification or removal of anything that could have an effect on IT services.
■ **RFC** A request for change – a formal proposal for a change to be made. It includes details of the proposed change, and may be recorded on paper or electronically.
■ **Change record** A record containing the details of a change. Each change record contains all the required information about a change, including information from the RFC, and is used to manage the lifecycle of that change.

4.2.4.4 Change models

A change model is a way of predefining steps to handle a particular type of change. Support tools can be configured to manage the required activities. The change model includes:

- Steps that should be taken to handle the change
- Responsibilities for each step, including identification of change authorities
- Timescales and thresholds for completion of activities
- Escalation procedures.

4.2.4.5 Change proposals

Major changes that involve significant cost, risk or organizational impact will usually be initiated through SPM. A change proposal is used to communicate a high-level description of the change. The change proposal should include:

- A high-level description of the service, including outcomes, utility and warranty
- A business case including risks, issues, alternatives, budget and financial expectations
- An outline schedule for design and implementation.

When the change proposal is authorized, the change schedule is updated to include outline implementation dates.

4.2.4.6 Standard changes

A standard change is a change for which the approach is pre-authorized. Every standard change has a change model that defines the steps to follow, including how the change should be logged, managed and implemented. For each standard change:

- There is a defined trigger to initiate the change, for example a service request
- The tasks are well known, documented and proven
- Budgetary approval is predefined or within the control of the change requester
- The risk is low and well understood.

4.2.4.7 Remediation planning

Every change should have a remediation plan stating what will be done if the change is not successful. If the change cannot be backed out then an alternative approach to remediation is required.

Change plans should include milestones and triggers for remediation to ensure that there is sufficient time in the change window if remediation is needed.

4.2.5 Process activities, methods and techniques

Figure 4.1 shows an example of a process flow for a normal change.

Figure 4.1 Example of a process flow for a normal change

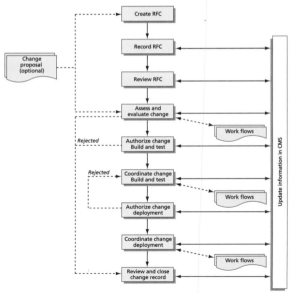

4.2.5.1　Create and record the RFC
- RFC is completed by someone from the business or IT.
- Change record is created, ideally on an integrated service management tool.

4.2.5.2　Review the RFC
- Changes are rejected if they are totally impractical, or are duplicates of earlier RFCs, or if the RFC is not complete.

4.2.5.3　Assess and evaluate the change
- Criteria are used to decide if evaluation should be by a formal change evaluation process or by a less formal approach
- The seven Rs of change management may be used to help ensure that required information is considered
  - Who **raised** the change?
  - What is the **reason** for the change?
  - What is the **return** required from the change?
  - What are the **risks** involved in the change?
  - What **resources** are required to deliver the change?
  - Who is **responsible** for the build, test and implementation of the change?
  - What is the **relationship** between this change and other changes?

4.2.5.4　Authorize change build and test
- Change authority is assigned based on defined criteria, such as anticipated risk, financial implications and scope of the change.
- Formal authorization to build and test the change is obtained from the change authority.

4.2.5.5　Coordinate change build and test
- The authorized change is passed to the relevant technical group, typically as a work order.

- If the change is part of a release then this is coordinated by release and deployment management.

4.2.5.6   Authorize change deployment

- Evaluate the change build and test before authorizing deployment.
- If this is a significant change then there should be an interim change evaluation report.
- If the change is not authorized then it may return to the previous step for re-work.

4.2.5.7   Coordinate change deployment

- Each deployment must be authorized by the change authority.
- Deployment should be scheduled for least impact on the business.
- This could require one RFC for each deployment, or a single RFC with multiple authorization stages.
- If the change is part of a release then this is coordinated by release and deployment management.

4.2.5.8   Review and close change record

- Evaluate the change to see if actual performance is acceptable.
- Gain stakeholder agreement before closing the change.
- Identify opportunities for improvement.

4.2.6   Triggers, inputs, outputs and interfaces

Triggers for change management could come from many places including:

- Strategic changes required by legal, regulatory or organizational change, or updates to the service portfolio
- Changes to individual services, to improve service utilities or warranties
- Operational changes such as password resets or access requests.

Inputs to change management include:

- Policy and strategy for change and release
- RFCs and change proposals
- Plans – change, transition, release, test, evaluation and remediation
- Current change schedule and projected service outage (PSO)
- Evaluation reports and interim evaluation reports
- Assets and CIs
- Test results and test reports
- Configuration baseline.

Outputs from change management include:

- Rejected and cancelled RFCs
- Authorized changes and change proposals
- Change to the services or infrastructure resulting from authorized changes
- New, changed or disposed CIs
- Revised change schedule and PSO
- Change documents, records and reports.

Interfaces with change management include

- **Transition planning and support** Provides coordination for all service transitions.
- **Release and deployment management** Change management must be integrated with release and deployment management to provide clear boundaries, dependencies and rules.
- **Change evaluation** Change management must be tightly integrated with change evaluation. There must be clear criteria to determine which changes need formal evaluation.
- **SACM** Change management works closely with SACM to obtain data about CIs and to provide updates to the CMS.
- **SPM** Prioritizes and charters strategic changes, and submits change proposals for these. Some change requests require

analysis by SPM, potentially adding to the service pipeline. Each organization should define criteria for deciding which requests are managed as part of change management and which are passed to SPM.

■ **Business change management** Change management must be involved with the business change management process and with programme and project management.

■ **Organizational change management** If a group or process is responsible for organizational and stakeholder change management then change management should work closely with them.

4.2.7 Critical success factors and key performance indicators

Examples of CSFs and KPIs for change management include:

■ **CSF** Responding to business and IT requests for change
 - **KPI** Average time to implement meets SLA targets
 - **KPI** Increase in stakeholder satisfaction scores for change management
■ **CSF** Optimizing overall business risk
 - **KPI** Increase in change success rate
 - **KPI** Reduction in number of unauthorized changes identified
 - **KPI** Reduction in number of incidents attributed to changes
■ **CSF** Ensuring that changes to CIs are well managed
 - **KPI** Reduction in audit compliance issues for change management
 - **KPI** Reduction in discrepancies found by SACM verification and audit.

4.2.8 Challenges and risks

Challenges to change management include:

■ Ensuring that every change is recorded and managed.

- Ensuring that change management is seen to facilitate change, rather than to introduce delays
- In organizations where change management only covers operational change, migration to a true change management process that becomes involved early enough in the service lifecycle can be difficult
- In large organizations there can be a significant challenge to agree and document the many levels of change authority and to communicate between these.

Risks to change management include:

- Lack of commitment to change management by the business or IT
- Implementation of changes without the use of change management
- Change assessment that is just box-ticking, without real consideration of risks, costs and benefits
- Insufficient time being allowed for assessment or implementation
- Lack of clarity on how change management should interact with release and deployment management, SACM, project management or service design.

4.3 SERVICE ASSET AND CONFIGURATION MANAGEMENT

4.3.1 Purpose and objectives

The purpose of the SACM process is to ensure that the assets required to deliver services are properly controlled, and that accurate and reliable information about those assets is available when and where it is needed. This information includes details of how the assets have been configured and the relationships between assets

The objectives of SACM are to:

- Ensure that assets are identified, controlled and cared for throughout their lifecycle
- Identify, control, record, report, audit and verify CIs, including attributes and relationships
- Work with change management to account for, manage and protect the integrity of CIs through the service lifecycle
- Ensure the integrity of CIs by maintaining an accurate and complete CMS
- Support efficient and effective service management by providing accurate configuration information.

4.3.2 Scope

Service assets that need to be managed in order to deliver services are known as configuration items (CIs). The scope of SACM includes management of the complete lifecycle of every CI. The scope includes interfaces to other service providers where there are assets and CIs that need to be controlled.

Fixed asset management maintains an asset register, which records financial information about all of the organization's fixed assets. Fixed asset management is not usually under the control of the same business unit as IT services, but the SACM process must provide proper care for fixed assets under the control of IT. Data from the asset register may be integrated with the CMS to provide a more complete view of the CIs.

4.3.3 Value to business

Optimizing the performance of service assets and configurations improves overall service performance and optimizes costs and risks.

SACM provides representations of a service, release or environment that enables:

- Better planning and delivery of changes and releases
- Resolution of incidents and problems within service level targets
- Delivery of service levels and warranties
- Better adherence to standards, legal and regulatory obligations
- More business opportunities, as the service provider is able to demonstrate control of assets and services
- Traceability of changes from requirements
- The ability to identify the costs of a service
- Reduced cost and time to discover configuration information
- Proper stewardship of fixed assets that are under the control of the service provider.

4.3.4 Policies, principles and basic concepts

It is important to distinguish between service assets, CIs and configuration records:

- **Service asset** Any resource or capability that could contribute to the delivery of a service. Examples include a virtual server, a physical server, or knowledge in the head of a manager.
- **CI** A service asset that needs to be managed in order to deliver an IT service. All CIs are service assets, but many service assets are not CIs. Examples of CIs are a server or a software licence.
- **Configuration record** A set of attributes and relationships about a CI. Configuration records are stored in a configuration management database (CMDB) and managed with a CMS.
- **CMS** A set of tools, data and information that supports SACM. It is part of the service knowledge management system (SKMS) and includes tools for collecting, storing, managing, updating, analysing and presenting data about CIs and their relationships. The CMS may also include information about incidents, problems, known errors, changes and releases.

- **SKMS** A set of tools and databases used to manage knowledge, information and data. Many CIs are stored in the SKMS – for example, a service level agreement, a report template or a definitive media library.

SACM delivers a model of the services, assets and infrastructure by recording the relationships between CIs. This model enables other processes to access information, for example to assess the impact and cause of incidents and problems, or to plan and design new or changed services.

SACM should be applied at a detailed level where the service provider requires more control, but should only include attributes or relationships that create more value than it costs to maintain them.

A **configuration baseline** is the configuration of a service or other CI that has been formally agreed. It can only be changed through formal procedures, and provides the basis for configuration audit, for back-out, or to build a specific version.

Fixed assets are assets which have financial value, can be used to help create products or services and have a long-term useful life. These may include CIs such as data centres, power distribution, servers, and software licences. Most organizations have a fixed asset management process that manages these, but the service provider is responsible for protecting assets in line with organizational policies.

The **definitive media library (DML)** is the secure library in which definitive authorized versions of media CIs are stored and protected. The DML may consist of one or more software libraries or file-storage areas, separate from development, test or live file store areas. Master copies of controlled documentation are also stored in the DML. The DML will also include a physical store, such as a fireproof safe.

Figure 4.2 Typical SACM activity model

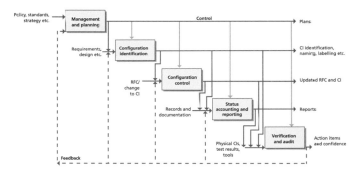

Software asset management (SAM) is responsible for the management of software, software licences and codes for activating software – whether these are installed on computer systems or held as copies that could be installed. SAM includes management, control and protection of software assets and the risks arising from their use. Effective SAM is dependent on the use of appropriate tools, including a CMS and DML.

4.3.5 Process activities, methods and techniques

High-level activities for SACM are shown in Figure 4.2.

4.3.5.1 Management and planning

The management team should decide what level of SACM is required and how this will be achieved. This is documented in a SACM plan. There may be a SACM plan for a project, service or group of services. These plans define specific SACM activities within the context of the SACM strategy.

4.3.5.2 Configuration identification

Configuration identification activities should:

- Define and document criteria for selecting CIs and their components
- Select the CIs and their components according to documented criteria
- Assign unique identifiers to CIs
- Specify the relevant attributes for each CI, including the owner
- Create a configuration model that describes the relationships of all CIs that contribute to the service.

4.3.5.3 Configuration control

Configuration control ensures there are control mechanisms over CIs and maintains a record of changes, versions, location and ownership. No CI should be added, modified, replaced or removed without the appropriate procedure being followed.

There are many procedures that can change a CI; these should be reviewed and aligned with the CI types.

4.3.5.4 Status accounting and reporting

Each CI will have one or more discrete states through which it can progress. For example, development or draft/approved/withdrawn. The method by which CIs move from one state to another should be defined. This will include defining the review and authorization required. At each status change, the CMS should be updated with the reason, time stamp and person who made the change.

Reports will be needed for SACM purposes. Such reports may cover individual CIs, a complete service or the full service portfolio.

4.3.5.5 Verification and audit

These activities include a series of reviews or audits to:

- Ensure that there is conformity between documented baselines and the actual environment
- Verify the existence of CIs and check that the records in the CMS match the physical infrastructure
- Check that required documentation is present for each release.

A rolling programme of configuration audits can encourage effective use of resources. The service desk checks that CIs (such as the desktop software that a caller is using) are as recorded in the CMS. Deviations are reported to SACM for investigation.

4.3.6 Triggers, inputs, outputs and interfaces

Triggers for SACM include:

- Updates from change management, or from release and deployment management
- Purchase orders and acquisitions
- Service requests.

Inputs to SACM include:

- Designs, plans and configurations from SDPs
- RFCs and work orders from change management
- Configuration information collected by tools and audits
- Information in the organization's fixed asset register.

Outputs from SACM include:

- New and updated configuration records
- Information for use in updating the fixed asset register
- Configuration snapshots and baselines
- Status reports, audit reports and other consolidated information.

As the single virtual repository of configuration data and information, SACM supports and interfaces with every other service management process and activity. These interfaces include:

- **Change management** Identifying the impact of proposed changes
- **Financial management** Capturing key financial information
- **ITSCM** Providing information about the assets on which services depend
- **Incident and problem management** Providing diagnostic information and other data to the service desk
- **Change management** and **release and deployment management** Understanding and capturing updates to infrastructure and services.

4.3.7 Critical success factors and key performance indicators

Examples of CSFs and KPIs for SACM include:

- **CSF** Accounting for, managing and protecting the integrity of CIs throughout the service lifecycle
  - **KPI** Reduced number of exceptions reported during configuration audits
- **CSF** Supporting efficient and effective service management by providing accurate configuration information at the right time
  - **KPI** Reduction in average time and cost of diagnosing and resolving incidents and problems (by type)
  - **KPI** Improved ratio of used licences against paid-for licences
- **CSF** Establishing and maintaining an accurate and complete CMS
  - **KPI** Improved audit compliance
  - **KPI** Fewer errors caused by people working with out-of-date information.

4.3.8 Challenges and risks

Challenges to SACM include:

- Persuading technical support staff to adopt a checking in/out policy

- Attracting and justifying funding for SACM
- An attitude of 'just collecting data because it is possible to do so'
- Lack of commitment and support from management.

Risks to successful SACM include:

- The temptation to consider it technically focused, rather than service- and business-focused
- The CMS becomes out of date due to the movement of assets by non-authorized staff
- Setting the scope too wide, causing excessive cost and effort for insufficient benefit
- Setting the scope too narrow, so that the process has too little benefit.

4.4 RELEASE AND DEPLOYMENT MANAGEMENT

4.4.1 Purpose and objectives

The purpose of the release and deployment management process is to plan, schedule and control the build, test and deployment of releases, and to deliver new functionality required by the business while protecting the integrity of existing services.

The objectives of release and deployment management are to:

- Define and agree release and deployment management plans
- Create and test release packages, and ensure that these are stored in a DML and recorded accurately in the CMS
- Deploy release packages from the DML following an agreed plan
- Ensure that all release packages can be tracked, installed, tested, verified and/or uninstalled or backed out if appropriate
- Ensure that organization and stakeholder change is managed
- Ensure that a new or changed service can deliver the agreed utility and warranty

- Record and manage deviations, risks and issues
- Ensure there is knowledge transfer to customers, users and IT staff.

4.4.2 Scope

The scope of release and deployment management includes the processes, systems and functions to package, build, test and deploy a release into live use, establish the service specified in the SDP, and formally hand the service over to the service operation functions. The scope includes all CIs required to implement a release, for example:

- Physical assets such as a server or network
- Virtual assets such as a virtual server or virtual storage
- Applications and software
- Training for users and IT staff
- Services, including all related contracts and agreements.

4.4.3 Value to business

Effective release and deployment management enables the service provider to add value to the business by:

- Delivering change, faster and at optimum cost and minimized risk
- Assuring that customers and users can use the new or changed service to support business goals
- Improving consistency in implementation approach
- Contributing to meeting auditable requirements for traceability.

Well-planned and implemented release and deployment management will make a significant difference to an organization's service costs.

4.4.4 Policies, principles and basic concepts

Release and deployment management policies can help the organization achieve the correct balance between cost, stability and agility. For some services it is important to maximize stability, even if this increases the time required to design and test changes. For other services it may be more important to support a rapidly changing business, and resources may be provided to ensure that this can be achieved.

A **release unit** comprises the components of an IT service that are normally released together. A release unit typically includes sufficient components to perform a useful function.

A **release package** is a set of CIs that will be built, tested and deployed together as a single release. Each release package will usually include one or more release units, or exceptionally may include only part of a release unit.

Releases should be uniquely identified according to a scheme defined in the release policy. The release identification should include a reference to the CIs that it represents and a version number.

Service design will define the approach to transition from the current service to the new or changed service. Each deployment will typically choose one from each of the following pairs of deployment options:

- **Big bang or phased approach** This determines whether the release is deployed to all users at the same time, or to different users at different times.
- **Push or pull approach** This determines whether the deployment is controlled from a central location, or whether users are free to deploy the software at a time they choose.

■ **Automation or manual methods** Automation helps to ensure repeatability and consistency, but the time required to provide a well-designed mechanism may not always be available or viable.

A release and deployment model should be used to help define all aspects of the release, including how it is built, entry and exit criteria for each stage, what environments will be used, template schedules, supporting systems, handover activities and roles and responsibilities.

4.4.5 Process activities, methods and techniques

High-level activities for release and deployment management are shown in Figure 4.3.

Figure 4.3 shows multiple points where an authorized change triggers release and deployment management activity. This does not require a separate RFC at each stage. Some organizations manage a whole release with a single change request and separate authorization at each stage; other organizations require a separate RFC for each stage. Both of these approaches are acceptable.

Figure 4.3 Phases of release and deployment management

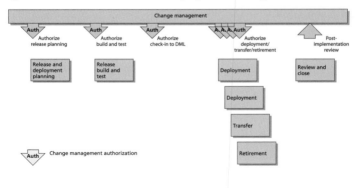

4.4.5.1 Release and deployment planning

Plans for creating and deploying the release are created. This phase starts with change management authorization to plan a release and ends with change management authorization to create the release. Most of this activity is carried out during the service design stage of the service lifecycle, and the design coordination process ensures that these plans are documented as part of the SDP.

4.4.5.2 Release build and test

The release package is built and tested and software components are checked into the DML. This phase starts with change management authorization to build the release and ends with change management authorization for the baselined release package to be checked into the DML by SACM. This phase only happens once for each release.

4.4.5.3 Deployment

The release package in the DML is deployed to the live environment. This phase starts with change management authorization to deploy the release package and ends with handover to the service operation functions and early life support. There may be many deployment phases for each release.

A pilot can be used to detect if any elements of the service do not deliver as required and to identify service management gaps/issues that put the service or the customer's business at risk. It does not need to cover all service functionality, but will focus on areas of risk and perform enough of the service to determine if it will work sufficiently well in deployment. As far as possible it should check that the utilities are fit for purpose and that the warranties are fit for use.

Formal handover to the service operation functions happens in two stages. At the beginning of early life support there is formal notification that the service is in live use. At the end of early life support there is formal notification that SLAs are now being enforced and the service is fully operational.

The service is monitored in early life support until the exit criteria are achieved; this will be when:

- Users can use the service effectively and efficiently
- Service owners and process owners are committed to manage and operate the service
- Service levels and performance standards are being consistently achieved
- SLAs and any other agreements are finalized and signed off
- Training and knowledge transfer activities are completed.

4.4.5.4 Review and close

Experience and feedback are captured, performance targets and achievements are reviewed and lessons are learned.

4.4.6 Triggers, inputs, outputs and interfaces

Triggers for release and deployment management include:

- Release and deployment management starts with receipt of an authorized change to plan, build and test a release package.
- Deployment starts with receipt of an authorized change to deploy a release package to a target group or environment.

Inputs to release and deployment management include:

- Authorized change
- SDP including:
  - Service charter that defines expected utility, warranty, outline budgets and timescales
  - Service models
  - SAC
- Acquired service assets and components and their documentation

- Service management and operations plans and standards
- Technology and procurement standards and catalogues
- Release policy and release design from service design
- Release and deployment models
- Entry and exit criteria for each stage.

Outputs from release and deployment management include:

- New, changed or retired services, documentation and plans
- SLA, underpinning operational level agreements (OLAs) and contracts
- New or changed service reports
- Tested continuity plans and updated capacity plans
- CMS updates
- Baselined release package checked in to the DML and ready for future deployments.

Interfaces with release and deployment management include:

- **Design coordination** Creates the SDP that defines the new service. Plans and packages should be developed and documented during service design, and design coordination ensures that these are documented in the SDP.
- **Transition planning and support** Provides the framework for release and deployment management to operate in, and transition plans provide the context for release and deployment plans.
- **Change management** Provides authorization for work done by release and deployment management, and release and deployment management provides the execution of many changes. Release and deployment plans are a significant part of the change schedule, and these must be managed together.
- **SACM** Release and deployment management depends on data and information in the CMS, and provides many updates to the CMS.

■ **Service validation and testing** Release and deployment management must coordinate with service validation and testing, to ensure that testing is carried out when necessary, and that builds are available when required.

4.4.7 Critical success factors and key performance indicators

Examples of CSFs and KPIs for release and deployment management include:

■ **CSF** Defining and agreeing release plans with customers and stakeholders
  – **KPI** Increased number and percentage of releases that meet customer expectations for cost, time and quality
■ **CSF** Ensuring integrity of a release package and its constituent components
  – **KPI** Reduced number of CMS and DML audit failures
  – **KPI** Reduced number of deployments from sources other than the DML
  – **KPI** Reduced number of incidents due to incorrect components being deployed
■ **CSF** Ensuring that new or changed services can deliver agreed utility and warranty
  – **KPI** Reduced variance from agreed service performance
  – **KPI** Increased customer and user satisfaction
■ **CSF** Ensuring that there is appropriate knowledge transfer
  – **KPI** Reduced number of incidents categorized as 'user knowledge'
  – **KPI** Increased score in satisfaction surveys for release and deployment management.

4.4.8 Challenges and risks

Challenges for release and deployment management include:

- Developing standard performance measures across projects and suppliers
- Dealing with inaccurate estimated delivery dates from projects and suppliers
- Understanding different stakeholder perspectives
- Building a thorough understanding of risks and encouraging a risk management culture.

Risks to successful release and deployment management include:

- Poorly defined scope or understanding of dependencies
- Using staff who are not dedicated to release and deployment management
- Failing to use release and deployment management for service retirement
- Shortage of finances
- Organizational change affecting employee morale
- Unclear expectations/objectives from stakeholders
- Failure of suppliers to meet contractual obligations
- Inadequate 'back-out' or 'contingency' plan if sourcing/partnering fails
- Inadequate design.

4.5 SERVICE VALIDATION AND TESTING

4.5.1 Purpose and objectives

The purpose of the service validation and testing process is to ensure that a new or changed IT service matches its design specification and will meet the needs of the business.

The objectives of service validation and testing are to:

■ Provide confidence that a new or changed service will deliver outcomes and value for customers within projected costs, capacity and constraints
■ Validate that a service is 'fit for purpose' – it will deliver the required utility
■ Provide assurance that a service is 'fit for use' – it will deliver the agreed warranty
■ Confirm that customer and stakeholder requirements are correctly defined
■ Identify, assess and address issues, errors and risks.

4.5.2 Scope

Service validation and testing can be used throughout the service lifecycle to quality assure any aspect of a service and the service providers' capability, resources and capacity to deliver the service. Service provider interface definitions define the boundaries of the service to be tested.

Testing is equally applicable to in-house or developed services, hardware, software or knowledge-based services. It includes the testing of new or changed services or service components and examines the behaviour of these in the target environment.

4.5.3 Value to business

Service failures can harm the service provider's business and the customer's assets and result in outcomes such as loss of reputation, loss of money, loss of time, injury and death. Key values to the business and customers from service testing and validation are:

■ Confidence that a new or changed service will deliver the value and outcomes required of it
■ Greater understanding of the risks.

4.5.4 Policies, principles and basic concepts

Typical service validation and testing policy statements might include:

- Tests must be designed and carried out by people who have not been involved in other design or development activities.
- Before the start of testing, test pass/fail criteria must be documented in an SDP and every test environment must be restored to a known state.
- Service validation and testing should maintain a reusable library of test models, test cases, test scripts and test data.
- Testing should be integrated into the project and service lifecycle.
- A risk-based testing approach should be adopted, aimed at reducing risk to the service and the customer's business.

Service validation and testing is also affected by policies from many other areas of service management, including the service quality policy, risk policy, service transition policy, release policy and change management policy.

A test model ensures that testing is executed consistently in a repeatable way that is effective and efficient. Test scripts define the test conditions, expected results and test cycles.

4.5.5 Process activities, methods and techniques

The testing process is shown in Figure 4.4. The test activities may not be undertaken in sequence. Several activities may be done in parallel, e.g. test execution can begin before all the test design is complete.

Figure 4.4 Example of a validation and testing process

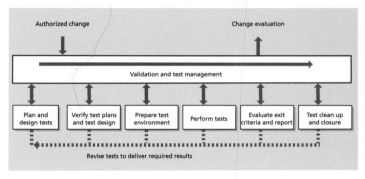

4.5.5.1 Plan and design tests
Test-planning activities start early in the service lifecycle and include:

- Resourcing (hardware, networking, staff, customers etc.)
- Supporting services (access, security, communications etc.)
- Schedule (milestones, handover, delivery)
- Budgets and funding.

4.5.5.2 Verify test plans and test design
To ensure that:

- Test model delivers appropriate coverage for the risks
- Test model covers key integration aspects and interfaces
- Test scripts are accurate and complete.

4.5.5.3 Prepare test environment
Capture a configuration baseline of the initial test environment.

4.5.5.4 Perform tests
- Use manual or automated procedures
- Record test findings

- Document reasons for any failures
- Resolve any incidents or issues if possible and retest.

4.5.5.5 Evaluate exit criteria and report

Compare actual to expected results.

4.5.5.6 Test clean up and closure

Clean up or initialize the test environment and identify opportunities for improvement.

4.5.6 Triggers, inputs, outputs and interfaces

The trigger for testing is a scheduled activity on a release plan, test plan or quality assurance plan.

Inputs to service validation and testing include:

- An SDP, which includes:
  - The service charter, describing utility and warranty, outline budgets and timescales
  - SAC
  - Test conditions and expected results
- RFCs, which specify the changes to be tested.

Outputs from service validation and testing include:

- Test report, delivered to change management or change evaluation
- Updated data, information and knowledge in the SKMS
- Test incidents, problems and error records
- Entries in the continual service improvement (CSI) register for potential improvements.

Interfaces with service validation and testing include:

- **Release and deployment management** Testing supports all steps of release and deployment management. Release and deployment management is responsible for ensuring that appropriate testing takes place.

- **Change evaluation** The output of service validation and testing is a key input to change evaluation.
- **Design coordination** To ensure that designs are testable and provide support in creating the SDP.

4.5.7 Critical success factors and key performance indicators

Examples of CSFs and KPIs for service validation and testing include:

- **CSF** Understanding stakeholder perspectives
    - **KPI** Roles and responsibilities for impact assessment and test activities have been agreed and documented
    - **KPI** Increase in satisfaction ratings in stakeholder survey of the service validation and testing process
- **CSF** Building a thorough understanding of risks
    - **KPI** Reduction in the impact of incidents and errors for newly transitioned services
    - **KPI** Increased number of risks identified in service design or early in service transition compared to those detected during or after testing
- **CSF** Encouraging a risk management culture
    - **KPI** Increase in the number of people who identify risks for new or changed services
- **CSF** Achieving a balance between cost and effectiveness of testing
    - **KPI** Reduced variance between test budget and test expenditure
    - **KPI** Reduced cost of fixing errors, due to earlier detection
    - **KPI** Reduction in business impact due to delays in testing.

4.5.8 Challenges and risks

The most frequent challenges for service validation and testing are based on lack of respect and understanding for testing, and lack of funding.

Risks to successful service validation and testing include:

- Unclear expectations/objectives
- Lack of understanding of the risks, resulting in testing that is not targeted at critical elements
- Resource shortages (e.g. users, support staff), which introduce delays and have an impact on other service transitions.

4.6 CHANGE EVALUATION

4.6.1 Purpose and objectives

The purpose of the change evaluation process is to provide a consistent and standardized means of determining the performance of a service change in the context of likely impacts on business outcomes, and on existing and proposed services and IT infrastructure. The actual performance of a change is assessed against its predicted performance. Risks and issues related to the change are identified and managed.

The objectives of change evaluation are to:

- Set stakeholder expectations correctly
- Evaluate the intended effects of a change and as much of the unintended effects as is reasonably practical
- Provide good-quality outputs so that change management can expedite an effective decision about whether or not a change is to be authorized.

4.6.2 Scope

Every change must be authorized at various points in its lifecycle; for example before build and test, before check-in to the DML and before deployment. Evaluation is required before each of these authorizations, to provide the change authority with advice and guidance.

This change evaluation process describes formal evaluation that is suitable for use when significant changes are being evaluated. Each organization must decide which changes should use this formal change evaluation, and which can be evaluated as part of the change management process. This decision should be documented in change models used to manage each type of change.

4.6.3 Value to business

Change evaluation will establish the use made of resources in terms of delivered benefit, and this information will allow a more accurate focus on value in service development and change management. There is a great deal of intelligence that continual service improvement can take from change evaluation to inform future improvements to the process of change and the predictions and measurement of change performance.

4.6.4 Policies, principles and basic concepts

The following examples of policies apply to the change evaluation process:

- Service designs or service changes will be evaluated before being transitioned.
- Every change must be evaluated, but only significant changes will use the formal change evaluation process; criteria must be defined to identify which changes are in scope of this process.
- Change evaluation will identify risks and issues related to the service being changed, and to any other services or shared infrastructure.
- Any deviation from predicted to actual performance will be managed by the customer accepting the change, rejecting the change, or requiring a new change to be implemented. *Note:* The term 'performance' is used in change evaluation to mean the utilities and warranties for the service.

As far as is reasonably practical, the unintended as well as the intended effects of a change should be identified and their consequences understood and considered.

The change evaluation process uses the Plan-Do-Check-Act (PDCA) model to ensure consistency across all evaluations. Each evaluation is planned and then carried out in multiple stages, the results of the evaluation are checked and actions are taken to resolve any issues found.

4.6.5 Process activities, methods and techniques

High-level activities for change evaluation are shown in Figure 4.5.

Figure 4.5 Change evaluation process flow

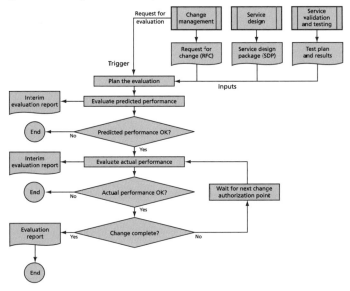

4.6.5.1   Evaluation planning

Evaluation should be carried out from a number of perspectives to ensure that unintended effects of the change are understood, as well as intended effects:

- **Understanding the intended effect of a change** Details of the customer requirements and the SDP are analysed.
- **Understanding the unintended effect of a change** One of the most effective ways of identifying these is by discussion with all stakeholders.

4.6.5.2   Evaluation of predicted performance

Risk assessment is carried out and an interim evaluation report is sent to change management. If change evaluation recommends that the change should not proceed, then activities end – pending a decision from change management. If the recommendation is to proceed with the change, then evaluation activities pause to wait for the next change authorization point.

4.6.5.3   Evaluation of actual performance

The extent to which actual performance can be evaluated depends on how far through the change lifecycle the evaluation is performed. The results of this evaluation are sent to change management in an interim evaluation report. After the change has been implemented an evaluation report is sent to change management.

4.6.6   Triggers, inputs, outputs and interfaces

The trigger for change evaluation is receipt of a request for evaluation from change management.

Inputs to change evaluation include:

- SDP, including service charter and SAC

- Change proposal, RFC, change record and detailed change documentation
- Discussions with stakeholders
- Test results and report.

Outputs from change evaluation include:

- Interim evaluation report(s) and evaluation report.

Interfaces with change evaluation include:

- **Transition planning and support** To ensure that appropriate resources are available and that each transition is well managed.
- **Change management** There must be agreement on which changes require formal evaluation. Change management provides the trigger for change evaluation, and evaluation reports are delivered to change management.
- **Design coordination** Provides the SDP, which includes information about the service.
- **Service level management and business relationship management** Provide information about impact of issues, and help to obtain customer resources to assist with the evaluation.
- **Service validation and test** Provides test results.

4.6.7 Critical success factors and key performance indicators

Examples of CSFs and KPIs for change evaluation include:

- **CSF** Stakeholders have a good understanding of expected performance
  - **KPI** Reduced number of incidents for new or changed services due to failure to deliver expected utility or warranty
  - **KPI** Increased stakeholder satisfaction with new or changed services as measured in customer surveys
- **CSF** Change management has good-quality evaluations to help them make correct decisions

- **KPI** Increased percentage of evaluations delivered by agreed times
- **KPI** Reduced number of changes backed out due to unexpected failures.

4.6.8 Challenges and risks

Challenges to change evaluation include:

- Developing standard performance measures and methods across projects and suppliers
- Understanding different stakeholder perspectives
- Understanding the balance between managing risk and taking risks, and encouraging a risk management culture
- Building a thorough understanding of risks that have impacted or may impact transition of services.

Risks to change evaluation include:

- Lack of clear criteria for when change evaluation should be used
- Unrealistic expectations of the time required
- Personnel with insufficient experience or authority
- Projects and suppliers estimating delivery dates inaccurately.

4.7 KNOWLEDGE MANAGEMENT

4.7.1 Purpose and objectives

The purpose of the knowledge management process is to share perspectives, ideas, experience and information; to ensure that these are available in the right place at the right time to enable informed decisions; and to improve efficiency by reducing the need to rediscover knowledge.

The objectives of knowledge management are to:

- Improve decision-making by ensuring that reliable knowledge, information and data are available
- Enable the service provider to be more efficient and improve quality of service, increase satisfaction and reduce the cost of service
- Maintain an SKMS that provides controlled access to appropriate knowledge, information and data
- Gather, analyse, store, share, use and maintain knowledge, information and data throughout the service provider organization.

4.7.2 Scope

Knowledge management is a lifecycle-wide process that is relevant to all lifecycle stages.

Knowledge management includes management of knowledge, and also management of the information and data from which that knowledge derives.

4.7.3 Value to business

Successful management of data, information and knowledge will deliver:

- Conformance with legal and other requirements
- Documented requirements for retention of each category of data, information and knowledge
- Data, information and knowledge that is current, complete and valid, and therefore easily usable by the organization
- Disposal of data, information and knowledge as required.

Knowledge management adds value to all stages of the service lifecycle by providing secure and controlled access to the knowledge, information and data that is needed to manage and deliver services.

4.7.4 Policies, principles and basic concepts

Typical knowledge management policies might include the following:

- Knowledge and information needed to support services will be stored in a way that allows this to be accessed by staff when and where needed.
- All policies, plans and processes must be reviewed at least once per year.
- All knowledge and information should be created, reviewed, approved, maintained, controlled and disposed of following a formal documented process.

Data is a set of discrete facts. Most organizations capture significant amounts of data in highly structured databases such as a CMDB.

Information comes from providing context to data. Information is typically semi-structured, in documents, email and multimedia.

Knowledge is composed of experiences, ideas, insights, values and judgements. People gain knowledge from their own and their peers' expertise, as well as from analysis of information and data.

Wisdom makes use of knowledge to create value through correct and well-informed decisions.

An **SKMS** is a set of tools and databases that is used to manage knowledge, information and data. The SKMS includes the CMS, as well as other databases and information systems. The SKMS includes tools for collecting, storing, managing, updating, analysing and presenting all the knowledge, information and data needed to manage the lifecycle of IT services.

Figure 4.6 shows data recorded in a CMDB, and feeding through the CMS into the SKMS.

Figure 4.6 Relationship of the CMDB, the CMS and the SKMS

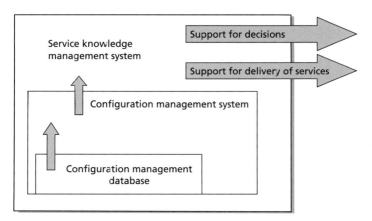

The SKMS will contain many different types of data, information and knowledge. Examples of items that should be stored in an SKMS include:

■ The service portfolio
■ The CMS and DML
■ SLAs, contracts and OLAs
■ Business plans
■ The CSI register
■ Capacity, availability and service continuity plans
■ Service reports
■ Web-based training courses.

4.7.5 Process activities, methods and techniques

4.7.5.1 Knowledge management strategy

An overall strategy for knowledge management is required to address:

- Governance, including software asset management, Sarbanes-Oxley, ISO/IEC 20000, ISO/IEC 38500 and COBIT if these are applicable
- Organizational changes and changes in roles and responsibilities
- Policies, processes, procedures and methods for knowledge management
- Technology and other resource requirements
- Performance measures.

The strategy should identify and plan for the capture of knowledge, information and data.

4.7.5.2 Knowledge transfer

Knowledge transfer is the activity through which one person or unit is able to learn from the experience, ideas or perspective of another. Knowledge transfer activities should include:

- Understanding of learning styles
- Use of visuals such as diagrams, images etc.
- Understanding how knowledge can be used to drive behaviour
- Seminars, webinars and documentation
- Journals and newsletters
- Discussion forums and social media.

4.7.5.3 Managing data, information and knowledge

This activity includes:

- Establishing data, information and knowledge requirements
- Defining the information architecture

- Establishing data, information and knowledge management procedures
- Evaluation and improvement.

4.7.6 Triggers, inputs, outputs and interfaces

Knowledge management has many triggers, relating to every requirement for storing, maintaining or using knowledge, information or data within the organization. For example:

- Storage of minutes of meetings
- Updates to the service catalogue or service portfolio
- Modification of a service design package
- Creation of a customer report.

Inputs to knowledge management include all knowledge, information and data used by the service provider, as well as relevant business data.

The key output of knowledge management is the knowledge required to make decisions and to manage the IT services, maintained within an SKMS.

Knowledge management has interfaces to every other service management process in every stage of the service lifecycle. The SKMS can only be effective if all processes and activities use it to store and manage their information and data.

4.7.7 Critical success factors and key performance indicators

Examples of CSFs and KPIs for knowledge management include:

- **CSF** Availability of knowledge and information to support decision-making
    - **KPI** Increased number of accesses to the SKMS by managers
    - **KPI** Increased percentage of SKMS searches by managers that receive a rating of 'good'

■ **CSF** Reduced dependency on personnel for knowledge.
  - **KPI** Increased number of times that the SKMS is accessed
  - **KPI** Increased percentage of SKMS searches that receive a rating of 'good' by the user
  - **KPI** Increased scores in regular customer satisfaction surveys for knowledge management.

4.7.8 Challenges and risks

Most organizations have knowledge, information and data that meet many of their needs, and it can be challenging to justify the effort needed to create an architecture for managing these.

Each team may own and manage information, and may see knowledge management as interfering in their work. The challenge is to help them understand the value that a holistic approach to knowledge management can bring.

Risks to knowledge management include:

■ Focusing on supporting tools, rather than on the creation of value
■ Insufficient understanding of what knowledge, information and data are needed
■ Spending too much effort on knowledge capture, with insufficient attention to knowledge transfer and re-use
■ Storing and sharing knowledge and information that are not up to date and relevant
■ Lack of support and commitment from stakeholders.

5 Organizing for service transition

There is no single best way to organize, and best practices described in ITIL need to be tailored to suit each situation, taking into account resource constraints and the size, nature and needs of the business and customers. The starting point for organizational design is service strategy.

Section 2.2.3 of this publication provides an overview of functions and roles.

5.1 FUNCTIONS

For service transition to be successful, an organization will need to define the roles and responsibilities required to undertake the processes and activities identified in this key element guide. These roles should be assigned to individuals, and an appropriate organization structure of teams, groups or functions established and managed.

Service transition does not define specific functions, but it does rely on the technical and application management functions described in *ITIL Service Operation*. Technical and application management provide resources and expertise to manage the whole service lifecycle, and roles within service transition may be performed by members of these functions.

5.2 ROLES

A number of roles need to be performed in support of service transition. The core ITIL publications provide guidelines and examples of role descriptions. In many cases roles will need to be combined or separated depending on the organizational context and size.

A RACI model can be used to define the roles and responsibilities in relation to processes and activities.

RACI is an acronym for:

- **Responsible** The person or people responsible for correct execution – for getting the job done.
- **Accountable** The person who has ownership of quality and the end result.
- **Consulted** The people who are consulted and whose opinions are sought. They have involvement through input of knowledge and information.
- **Informed** The people who are kept up to date on progress. They receive information about process execution and quality.

Only one person should be accountable for any process or individual activity, although several people may be responsible for executing parts of the activity.

Roles fall into two main categories – generic roles such as process manager and process owner, and specific roles that are involved within a particular lifecycle stage or process, such as a change administrator or knowledge management process owner.

5.2.1 Generic service owner role

The service owner is accountable for the delivery of a specific IT service and is responsible for the initiation, transition, maintenance and support of that service.

The service owner's responsibilities include:

- Working with business relationship management to ensure that the service provider can meet customer requirements
- Participating in negotiating service level agreements (SLAs) and operational level agreements (OLAs) relating to the service
- Ensuring that ongoing service delivery and support meet agreed customer requirements

- Ensuring consistent and appropriate communication with customer(s) for service-related enquiries and issues
- Representing the service across the organization, including at change advisory board (CAB) meetings
- Serving as the point of escalation (notification) for major incidents relating to the service
- Participating in internal and external service review meetings.

The service owner is responsible for continual improvement and the management of change affecting the service under their care.

5.2.2 Generic process owner role

The process owner role is accountable for ensuring that a process is fit for purpose, is performed according to agreed standards and meets the aims of the process definition. This role is often assigned to the same person who carries out the process manager role, but the two roles may be separate in larger organizations.

The process owner's accountabilities include:

- Sponsoring, designing and change managing the process and its metrics
- Defining appropriate policies and standards for the process, with periodic auditing to ensure compliance
- Providing process resources to support activities required throughout the service lifecycle
- Ensuring that process technicians understand their role and have the required knowledge to deliver the process
- Addressing issues with running the process
- Identifying enhancement and improvement opportunities and making improvements to the process.

5.2.3 Generic process manager role

The process manager role is accountable for operational management of a process. There may be several process managers for one process, for example covering different locations.

The process manager's accountabilities include:

- Working with the process owner to plan and coordinate all process activities
- Ensuring that all activities are carried out as required throughout the service lifecycle
- Appointing people to the required roles and managing assigned resources
- Monitoring and reporting on process performance
- Identifying opportunities for and making improvements to the process.

5.2.4 Generic process practitioner role

The process practitioner's responsibilities include:

- Carrying out one or more activities of a process
- Understanding how their role contributes to the overall delivery of service and creation of value for the business
- Ensuring that inputs, outputs and interfaces for their activities are correct
- Creating or updating records to show that activities have been carried out correctly.

5.2.5 Transition planning and support roles

Many organizations will have a person with the job title 'service transition manager'. This job typically combines the roles of transition planning and support process owner with transition planning and support process manager.

5.2.5.1 Transition planning and support process owner

Responsibilities typically include:

- Carrying out generic process owner role for transition planning and support
- Setting the scope and policies for service transition
- Overseeing the overall design of all service transition processes.

5.2.5.2 Transition planning and support process manager

Responsibilities typically include:

- Carrying out generic process manager role for transition planning and support
- Managing and coordinating functions involved in service transition
- Budgeting and accounting for service transition activities and resources
- Managing and coordinating requests for resources
- Coordinating activities across projects, suppliers and service teams.

5.2.5.3 Transition planning and support practitioner

Responsibilities typically include:

- Maintaining and integrating plans for specific service transitions
- Monitoring progress for changes, issues, risks and deviations
- Maintaining records and providing management information
- Communicating with stakeholders.

5.2.6 Change management roles

In many organizations there will be someone with the job title of change manager, who combines the roles of change management process owner, change management process manager and chair of a change advisory board (CAB).

5.2.6.1 Change management process owner

Responsibilities typically include:

- Carrying out the generic process owner role for change management
- Designing change authority hierarchy and criteria
- Designing change models and workflows
- Working with other process owners to ensure that there is an integrated approach to service transition.

5.2.6.2 Change management process manager

Responsibilities typically include:

- Carrying out the generic process manager role for change management
- Planning and managing support for change management tools and processes
- Maintaining the change schedule and projected service outage
- Coordinating interfaces between change management and other processes.

5.2.6.3 Change initiator

Many different people in the organization may carry out this role; it is not usually undertaken by people who work in change management. Responsibilities typically include:

- Completing and submitting a change proposal if appropriate
- Completing and submitting an RFC
- Attending CAB meetings to provide further information
- Reviewing changes when requested by change management.

5.2.6.4 Change practitioner

Responsibilities typically include:

- Verifying that RFCs are correctly completed and allocating them to change authorities based on defined criteria

- Communicating decisions of change authorities to affected parties
- Monitoring and reviewing activities
- Publishing the change schedule and projected service outage.

5.2.6.5   Change authority

Responsibilities typically include:

- Reviewing specific categories of RFC
- Formally authorizing changes at agreed points in the change lifecycle
- Participating in the change review before changes are closed.

5.2.6.6   CAB member

In many organizations, the CAB is the change authority for some categories of change. In other organizations the CAB is just an advisory body.

Responsibilities typically include:

- Circulating RFCs within their own group and coordinating feedback
- Reviewing RFCs and recommending whether they should be authorized
- Reviewing successful, failed and unauthorized changes
- Reviewing the change schedule and projected service outage.

5.2.6.7   CAB chair

Responsibilities typically include:

- Planning, scheduling, managing and chairing CAB meetings
- Selecting RFCs for review at CAB meetings
- Convening emergency change advisory board (ECAB) meetings
- Selecting successful and failed changes for review at CAB meetings.

5.2.7 Service asset and configuration management roles

5.2.7.1 SACM process owner

Responsibilities typically include:

- Carrying out the generic process owner role for SACM
- Agreeing and documenting scope for SACM
- Working with other process owners to ensure that there is an integrated approach to service transition.

5.2.7.2 SACM process manager

Responsibilities typically include:

- Carrying out the generic process manager role for SACM
- Being accountable for stewardship of fixed assets under the control of IT
- Defining and agreeing service assets that will be treated as CIs
- Ensuring that configuration data is available when and where needed
- Planning and managing support for SACM tools and processes
- Coordinating interfaces between SACM and other processes.

5.2.7.3 Configuration analyst

Responsibilities typically include:

- Supporting the process owner and process manager in creation of principles, processes and procedures
- Defining the structure of the CMS
- Training staff in SACM principles, processes and procedures
- Performing configuration audits.

5.2.7.4 Configuration librarian

Responsibilities typically include:

- Controlling the receipt, identification, storage and withdrawal of CIs

■ Maintaining status information on CIs and providing this as appropriate
■ Assisting in conducting configuration audits
■ Identifying, recording, storing and distributing issues relating to SACM.

5.2.8 Release and deployment management roles

5.2.8.1 Release and deployment management process owner

Responsibilities typically include:

■ Carrying out the generic process owner role for release and deployment management
■ Designing release models and workflows
■ Working with other process owners to ensure that there is an integrated approach to service transition.

5.2.8.2 Release and deployment management process manager

It is important that this role is separate from service validation and testing roles, to avoid conflicts of interest.

Responsibilities typically include:

■ Carrying out the generic process manager role for release and deployment management
■ Planning resources needed to build, test and deploy each release
■ Planning and managing support for release and deployment management tools and processes
■ Ensuring that change authorization is provided before activities which require this
■ Coordinating interfaces with other processes.

5.2.8.3 Release packaging and build practitioner

Responsibilities typically include:

- Helping to design the release package, during the service design stage
- Building and testing the release
- Establishing and reporting known errors and workarounds
- Providing input to support change authorization for check-in of the release.

5.2.8.4 Deployment practitioner

Responsibilities typically include:

- Helping to plan the deployment, during the service design stage
- Ensuring that all deployment activity has been authorized
- Carrying out the final physical delivery of the deployment
- Coordinating release documentation and communications.

5.2.8.5 Early life support practitioner

Responsibilities typically include:

- Providing support to assist the service desk
- Providing release acceptance for provision of initial support
- Adapting and perfecting documentation
- Monitoring incidents and problems
- Providing initial performance reporting and risk assessment.

5.2.8.6 Build and test environment manager

Responsibilities typically include:

- Ensuring that infrastructure and application are built to specification
- Planning acquisition, build, implementation and maintenance of infrastructure
- Ensuring that all components are from controlled sources
- Delivering appropriate documentation for build and test environments.

5.2.9 Service validation and testing roles

5.2.9.1 Service validation and testing process owner

Responsibilities typically include:

- Carrying out the generic process owner role for service validation and testing
- Defining the overall test strategy for the organization
- Working with other process owners to ensure that there is an integrated approach to service transition.

5.2.9.2 Service validation and testing process manager

It is important that this role is assigned to a different person from whoever is responsible for release and deployment management, to avoid conflicts of interest.

Responsibilities typically include:

- Carrying out the generic process manager role for service validation and testing
- Helping to design and plan testing during the service design stage
- Allocating and overseeing test resources
- Verifying tests conducted by other teams
- Providing management reporting.

5.2.9.3 Service validation and testing practitioner

Responsibilities typically include:

- Conducting tests
- Recording, analysing, diagnosing, reporting and managing testing
- Administering test assets and components.

5.2.9.4 Contribution of other roles to service validation and testing

A number of other roles play a significant part in service validation and testing. These include:

- **Change management personnel** Ensure that testing strategy and policy are applied to all changes
- **Developers/suppliers** Establish root cause of test failures
- **Service design personnel** Design tests as part of SDP
- **Customers and users** Perform acceptance testing.

5.2.10 Change evaluation roles

5.2.10.1 Change evaluation process owner

Responsibilities typically include:

- Carrying out the generic process owner role for the change evaluation process
- Working with other process owners to ensure that there is an integrated approach to service transition.

5.2.10.2 Change evaluation process manager

Responsibilities typically include:

- Carrying out the generic process manager role for change evaluation
- Planning and coordinating resources needed to evaluate changes
- Ensuring that evaluation reports and interim evaluation reports are delivered at required times.

5.2.10.3 Change evaluation process practitioner

Responsibilities typically include:

- Developing an evaluation plan as input to service validation and testing
- Establishing risks and issues
- Creating an evaluation report as input to change management.

5.2.11 Knowledge management roles

5.2.11.1 Knowledge management process owner
Responsibilities typically include:

- Carrying out the generic process owner role for knowledge management
- Creating the architecture for knowledge management.

5.2.11.2 Knowledge management process manager
Responsibilities typically include:

- Carrying out the generic process manager role for knowledge management
- Ensuring that knowledge items are accessible to those who need them
- Planning and managing support for tools and processes
- Encouraging people to contribute knowledge to the SKMS
- Advising business and IT personnel on knowledge management matters.

5.2.11.3 Knowledge management process practitioner
Responsibilities typically include:

- Identifying, controlling and storing information
- Maintaining controlled knowledge items to ensure that they are current, relevant and valid
- Ensuring that information is not duplicated.

5.2.11.4 Knowledge creator
This role may be carried out by many different people in the organization. Creation and sharing of knowledge is often written into the job descriptions of people in a wide variety of roles within IT and the business.

6 Implementing service transition

Service transition is rarely introduced into a new situation. The task for most service providers is to improve service transition, and the techniques and approaches described in *ITIL Continual Service Improvement* can be used for this.

The stages of introducing service transition will match that of other services, requiring justification (strategic considerations), design and then transition before running in normal mode (service operation).

It is not advisable to attempt to retrofit new service transition practices onto projects that are under way; the benefits from the improved practices are unlikely to outweigh the disruption.

The processes involved in the service transition stage of the service lifecycle are not independent of each other. The relationships between them are complex and it is not possible to design and implement them separately. A plan for introduction or improvement of service transition should be based on understanding how the processes fit together; roles and responsibilities of all the people; and matching the inputs, outputs and triggers of each process with steps in other processes.

6.1 IMPLEMENTING SERVICE TRANSITION IN A VIRTUAL OR CLOUD ENVIRONMENT

Organizations that are implementing virtualization or cloud architectures must consider the impact on service transition. These environments can be very dynamic, often requiring rapid provisioning of new virtual servers or migration of virtual servers between hosts to support changing workloads. It is likely that many activities will be automated – for example:

- Creation, deployment and retirement of virtual servers
- Adding physical resources to provide greater capacity
- Moving a virtual server from one physical server to another.

There will be a requirement for new CI types, release models, change models and standard changes. It is likely that tools, activities, authorities, roles and responsibilities will also be completely different. Change management and release and deployment management must be designed to work seamlessly across both physical and virtual servers, and the CMS must be able to reflect the complexity of the relationships.

In a different context, an organization that moves its services from a traditional insourced data centre to a public cloud may find that its SACM needs are greatly simplified. There is still a need to carry out SACM, but the CIs are likely to be at a much higher level.

7 Challenges, risks and critical success factors

7.1 CHALLENGES

Challenges to service transition include:

- Managing many contacts, interfaces, relationships and stakeholders
- Lack of integration of the processes and disciplines that impact service transition, e.g. finance, engineering, human resource management
- Achieving balance between stability and responsiveness
- Creating an environment that fosters standardization, simplification and knowledge sharing
- Enabling business change, and becoming part of business change programmes
- Establishing leaders to champion the changes and improvements
- Developing standard performance measures across projects and suppliers
- Ensuring that service transition time and budget are not impacted by events earlier in the service lifecycle (e.g. budget cuts)
- Understanding the balance between managing risk and taking risks.

7.2 RISKS

Risks to service transition include:

- Change in practices of existing projects that demotivate the workforce
- Alienation of key support and operations staff

- Excessive costs generated by overly risk-averse practices and plans
- Knowledge sharing (the wrong people may have access to information)
- Lack of maturity and integration of systems and tools resulting in people 'blaming' technology for other shortcomings
- Poor integration between processes
- Loss of productive hours, higher costs, loss of revenue or perhaps even business failure as a result of poor service transition processes.

7.3   CRITICAL SUCCESS FACTORS

Critical success factors for service transition might include:

- Understanding and managing the different stakeholder perspectives
- Clearly defined relationships and interfaces with programme and project management
- Integrating with the other service lifecycle stages, processes and disciplines
- Understanding dependencies
- Automating processes to eliminate errors and reduce the cycle time
- Creating and maintaining knowledge in a form that people can find and use
- Developing good-quality systems, tools, processes and procedures
- Developing a workforce with the necessary knowledge, skills, and culture
- Defining clear accountabilities, roles and responsibilities
- Building a thorough understanding of risks
- Being able to communicate attitude to risk and approach to risk management.

8 Key messages and lessons

Key messages and guidance when looking to implement service transition are as follows:

■ The scale of change is not important; what is important is understanding that all change should follow the ITIL service lifecycle to ensure delivery of the best possible benefit to the business.
■ Use previous experience to ensure that service transition practices and processes are constantly reviewed and improved; encode this experience in understandable service transition models and documentation that can be shared and re-used.
■ An organization with a mixture of centralized, distributed and localized infrastructure should consider piloting each type separately, as the extra cost and complications are worth it.

When designing service transition, consider how agreed policies, standards and legislation will constrain the design:

■ Communication is critical throughout any transition – both internally and externally – with customers, stakeholders and suppliers.
■ Although service transition practices should deliver a net benefit to the organization, nonetheless they do require funding, and the service transition strategy should address the source and control of financial provision.
■ Service transition needs to take a broad view across projects, transitions and releases to make the best use of available resources.
■ If implementing service transition into an organization means installing formal processes that were not there before, the cultural change is significant. Experience shows that staff working in change management, and even those evangelizing change among others, are potentially as resistant to change as anyone else.

When delivering business change that involves many different departments, ensure that ownership for each component of the overall service package is defined, and subsequent management responsibility is clear.

9 Related guidance

This chapter provides some information about other frameworks, best practices, models and quality systems that have synergy with the ITIL service lifecycle.

9.1 RISK ASSESSMENT AND MANAGEMENT

Risk may be defined as uncertainty of outcome, whether a positive opportunity or negative threat. Formal risk management enables better decision-making based on a sound understanding of risks and their likely impact.

A number of different methodologies, standards and frameworks have been developed for risk management. Each organization should determine the approach to risk management that is best suited to its needs and circumstances.

Approaches to risk management that should be considered include:

- Office of Government Commerce (2010). *Management of Risk: Guidance for Practitioners*. TSO, London.
- ISO 31000
- ISO/IEC 27001
- Risk IT[2]

9.2 ITIL GUIDANCE AND WEB SERVICES

ITIL is part of the Best Management Practice portfolio of best-practice guidance.

The Best Management Practice website (www.best-management-practice.com) includes news, reviews, case studies and white papers on ITIL and all other Best Management Practice guidance.

---

[2] With the publication of COBIT 5, Risk IT will be included within COBIT.

The ITIL official website (www.itil-officialsite.com) contains reliable, up-to-date information on ITIL – including information on accreditation and the ITIL software scheme for the endorsement of ITIL-based tools.

Details of the core ITIL publications are:

- Cabinet Office (2011). *ITIL Service Strategy*. TSO, London.
- Cabinet Office (2011). *ITIL Service Design*. TSO, London.
- Cabinet Office (2011). *ITIL Service Transition*. TSO, London.
- Cabinet Office (2011). *ITIL Service Operation*. TSO, London.
- Cabinet Office (2011). *ITIL Continual Service Improvement*. TSO, London.

The full ITIL glossary, in English and other languages, can be accessed through the ITIL official site at:

www.itil-officialsite.com/InternationalActivities/TranslatedGlossaries.aspx

The full range of ITIL-derived and complementary publications can be found in the publications library of the Best Management Practice website at:

www.best-management-practice.com/Publications-Library/IT-Service-Management-ITIL/

9.3 QUALITY MANAGEMENT SYSTEM

Quality management focuses on product/service quality as well as the quality assurance and control of processes. Total Quality Management (TQM) is a methodology for managing continual improvement by using a quality management system.

ISO 9000:2005 describes the fundamentals of quality management systems that are applicable to all organizations which need to demonstrate their ability to consistently provide products that meet requirements. ISO 9001:2008 specifies generic requirements for a quality management system.

9.4   GOVERNANCE OF IT

ISO 9004 (Managing for the sustained success of an organization – a quality management approach) provides guidance on governance for the board and top management of an organization.

ISO/IEC 38500 is the standard for corporate governance of IT. The purpose of this standard is to promote effective, efficient and acceptable use of IT in all organizations.

9.5   COBIT

The Control OBjectives for Information and related Technology (COBIT) is a governance and control framework for IT management created by ISACA and the IT Governance Institute (ITGI).

COBIT is positioned at a high level, is driven by business requirements, covers the full range of IT activities, and concentrates on *what* should be achieved rather than *how* to achieve effective governance, management and control. ITIL provides an organization with best-practice guidance on *how* to manage and improve its processes to deliver high-quality, cost-effective IT services.

Further information about COBIT is available at www.isaca.org and www.itgi.org

9.6   ISO/IEC 20000 SERVICE MANAGEMENT SERIES

ISO/IEC 20000 is an internationally recognized standard for ITSM covering service providers who manage and deliver IT-enabled services to internal or external customers. ISO/IEC 20000-1 is aligned with other ISO management systems standards such as ISO 9001 and ISO/IEC 27001.

One of the most common routes for an organization to achieve the requirements of ISO/IEC 20000 is by adopting ITIL best practices.

Further details can be found at www.iso.org or
www.isoiec20000certification.com

9.7 ENVIRONMENTAL MANAGEMENT AND GREEN/SUSTAINABLE IT

'Green IT' refers to environmentally sustainable computing where
the use and disposal of computers and printers are carried out in
sustainable ways that do not have a negative impact on the
environment.

The ISO 14001 series of standards for an environment management
system is designed to assure internal and external stakeholders that
the organization is an environmentally responsible organization.

Further details are available at www.iso.org

9.8 PROGRAMME AND PROJECT MANAGEMENT

The principles of programme management are key to delivering on
time and within budget. Best management practice in this area is
found in *Managing Successful Programmes* (MSP) (TSO, 2011).

Visit www.msp-officialsite.com for more information on MSP.

Portfolio, Programme and Project Offices (P3O) (TSO, 2008) is aimed
at helping organizations to establish and maintain appropriate
business support structures with proven roles and responsibilities.

Visit www.p3o-officialsite.com for more information on P3O.

Structured project management methods, such as PRINCE2 (PRojects
IN Controlled Environments) (TSO, 2009) or the Project Management
Body of Knowledge (PMBOK) developed by the Project
Management Institute (PMI), can be used when improving IT
services.

Visit www.prince-officialsite.com for more information on PRINCE2.

Visit www.pmi.org for more information on PMI and PMBOK.

9.9 SKILLS FRAMEWORK FOR THE INFORMATION AGE

The Skills Framework for the Information Age (SFIA) supports skills audit, planning future skill requirements, development programmes, standardization of job titles and functions, and resource allocation.

Visit www.sfia.org.uk for further details.

9.10 CARNEGIE MELLON: CMMI AND ESCM FRAMEWORK

The Capability Maturity Model Integration (CMMI) is a process improvement approach developed by the Software Engineering Institute (SEI) of Carnegie Mellon University. CMMI can be used to guide process improvement across a project, a division or an entire organization.

The eSourcing Capability Model for Service Providers (eSCM-SP) is a framework developed by ITSqc at Carnegie Mellon to improve the relationship between IT service providers and their customers.

For more information, see www.sei.cmu.edu/cmmi/

9.11 BALANCED SCORECARD

The balanced scorecard approach provides guidance for what companies should measure to provide a balanced view. The balanced scorecard suggests that the organization be viewed from four perspectives, and it is valuable to develop metrics, collect data and analyse the organization relative to each of these perspectives:

- The learning and growth perspective
- The business process perspective
- The customer perspective
- The financial perspective.

Further details are available through the balanced scorecard user community at www.scorecardsupport.com

9.12 SIX SIGMA

Six Sigma is a data-driven process improvement approach that supports continual improvement. The objective is to implement a measurement-oriented strategy focused on process improvement and defects reduction. A Six Sigma defect is defined as anything outside customer specifications.

There are two primary sub-methodologies within Six Sigma: DMAIC (Define, Measure, Analyse, Improve, Control) and DMADV (Define, Measure, Analyse, Design, Verify). DMAIC is an improvement method for existing processes for which performance does not meet expectations, or for which incremental improvements are desired. DMADV focuses on the creation of new processes.